IN THIS SERIES

Auto Racing

Baseball

Basketball

Football

Golf

Hockey

Lacrosse

Soccer

Tennis

Track and Field

Wrestling

THE COMPOSITE GUIDE

to **BASKETBALL**

DENNIS TUTTLE

CHELSEA HOUSE PUBLISHERS

Philadelphia

Produced by Choptank Syndicate, Inc.

Editor and Picture Researcher: Norman L. Macht
Production Coordinator and Editorial Assistant: Mary E. Hull
Design and Production: Lisa Hochstein
Cover Illustrator: Cliff Spohn
Cover Design: Keith Trego

First Printing

1 3 5 7 9 8 6 4 2

Library of Congress Cataloging-in-Publication Data

Tuttle, Dennis R.
        The composite guide to basketball / Dennis Tuttle.
            p. cm.— (The composite guide)
        Includes bibliographical references (p.) and index.
        Summary: Surveys the history of basketball, from its beginnings
    in a Massachusetts YMCA through its evolution into a professional
    sport to the modern era of highly paid superstars.
        ISBN 0-7910-4724-5
        1. Basketball—United States—History—Juvenile literature.
        2. National Basketball Association—History—Juvenile literature.
        [1. Basketball—History.] I. Title II. Series.
        GV885.1.T88 1997
        796.323'0973—dc21   97-31495
                                                                    CIP
                                                                     AC

CONTENTS

1 A LEGEND EMBELLISHED

The sickness that swept through his body kept Michael Jordan from eating, drinking, or even getting out of bed. Every time he tried to sit up, he became dizzy and nauseous. The stomach virus was so severe that 30 minutes before his Chicago Bulls were to play Game 5 of the 1997 NBA finals against the Utah Jazz, Jordan walked off the court during the shoot-around and threw up.

Any other player might have stayed in bed or watched from the bench. But Michael Jordan was like no other player. Throughout his glorious career, the highly competitive Jordan always answered the challenge—and few did it better.

Angered over criticism about a gambling trip he took to Atlantic City during the 1993 Eastern Conference finals against New York. Jordan torched the Knicks for 29 points, 10 rebounds, and 14 assists in the next game.

When he was 31, he tried to switch careers and become a baseball player. After a brief stint as a minor league outfielder for the Chicago White Sox, Jordan returned to the Bulls late in the 1995 season. He was terrible in his first game, scoring just 19 points. Critics said that, at age 33, he was too old, too slow, and out of shape. In his next game, he answered them by scoring 55 points.

When the Bulls played for the championship in 1996 against Seattle, Jordan was guarded by Gary Payton, among the best defensive players

Michael Jordan of the Chicago Bulls seemed always to rise above the crowd in big games. Here he soars past Knicks center Patrick Ewing for 2 of his 42 points in this 1990 game.

in the NBA. The Bulls won the series in six games, and Jordan was named Most Valuable Player.

By 1997, the Bulls were chasing history, hoping to create a dynasty rivaling the great Boston Celtics teams from 1956 to 1969 and the "Showtime" Los Angeles Lakers of the 1980s. The Bulls had won a record 72 games in 1995–96 and their fourth championship in six years. But the experts considered them too old to repeat in '97.

"I'm going to send Mike home this year," boasted All-Star center Shaquille O'Neal of the Lakers, who soon learned not to doubt Jordan's heart, soul, and spirit.

"There are two situations where you have to be especially careful with Michael," said Atlanta Hawks coach Lenny Wilkens, the NBA's all-time winningest coach. "When *he* thinks *he* has you in trouble, and when *you* think *you* have him in trouble."

Jordan's killer instinct was part of what made him the most famous basketball player in the world. He won seven consecutive scoring titles between 1986 and 1993. His acrobatic moves to the basket and ability to soar above defenders for jump shots, dunks, and finger-roll lay-ins defied belief.

But seeing was believing; his list of unforgettable performances seemed endless. After missing most of the 1986 season with a broken foot, he returned for the playoffs, scoring 49 points in the first game and a postseason-record 63 in Game 2, a 135–131 double overtime loss to Boston.

In 1989, with the Bulls trailing by a point with three seconds to play in Game 5 of the

Kids on playgrounds bit their tongues trying to imitate Michael Jordan's open-mouthed, tongue-waggling slams.

first-round series at Cleveland, Jordan took the inbounds pass, spun, and hit an 18-foot jumper from the top of the key at the buzzer to win, 101–100.

In Game 1 of the 1992 finals against Portland, he scored 35 first-half points, including six three-pointers. At one point he drained a shot, looked toward the sideline, turned his palms up, and shrugged, as if to say, "What can I tell you?" It all seemed so easy for him.

With the Bulls leading 106–105 in Game 4 of the 1993 NBA finals and just 30 seconds to play, Jordan put the game out of reach by driving the lane, scoring, getting fouled, and hitting the free throw. He finished with 55 points—half his team's total.

In Game 1 of the 1997 NBA finals, Jordan hit the game-winning shot at the buzzer as the Bulls rallied for a 97–94 win over the Jazz. Jordan finished with 31 points.

But now the Bulls faced the critical Game 5 with a Michael Jordan who could barely walk. Despite winning the first two games, the Bulls were in danger of being dethroned. Utah had won the next two at home to tie the series. If the Jazz took a 3–2 lead, the tired and worn-down Bulls would have a difficult time coming back.

Jordan moved slowly onto the court. During timeouts of the closely fought game, he plopped into a chair, his eyes glazed, his body feverish and dehydrated. But he refused to come out of the game.

Neither team could pull away through three quarters. It took 12 points by Jordan to get the Bulls to 87–87 with 25 seconds to play in the game. He had so little energy left he had to be held up by teammates during a break. But he took the final pass and hit a three-pointer that proved to be the game-winner in the Bulls' 90–88 victory. The revitalized Bulls went home and won Game 6 in another nail-biting contest to repeat as champions.

"I'm tired, I'm weak, but I've got the whole summer to recuperate," Jordan said. "It's been a fight. It's all guts, deep-down determination. There's been a lot of soul-searching. It's easy to sit back and say, 'I've given my best, I'm tired, somebody else has to do it.' But I didn't take that approach. I did whatever I could do. Every little inch of energy I have, I'm going to provide for this team. I didn't want to give up, no matter how sick I was, or how tired I was, or how low on energy I was."

Small wonder that Michael Jordan had become the greatest player in pro basketball history, a crown once worn by men named George Mikan, Wilt Chamberlain, Larry Bird, Magic Johnson, and Julius Erving.

2

PEACH BASKETS IN THE YMCA

Basketball is the only major sport born in America with no connection to any other game. In the winter of 1891, physical education students at the International YMCA Training School in Springfield, Massachusetts, became bored with indoor gymnastics and calisthenics. The school's director asked James Naismith, a part-time instructor, to invent an indoor game.

Naismith decided on a game involving a ball and goal. The janitor gave him two old peach baskets. Naismith climbed a ladder and nailed them into the opposite ends of the lower rail of the balcony of the gym, about 10 feet above the floor. He grabbed a soccer ball, outlined a few basic rules, and instructed his students that the idea of the game was to throw the ball into the baskets. To prevent injuries, he banned running with the ball.

Naismith divided his class of 18 students into two nine-player teams. The game was sloppy, disorganized, and rough, just the way a game would be that nobody had ever seen or played. But the students loved it. Within two weeks, more than 200 people were lining up outside the gym to play.

During Christmas break, many of the players introduced the game to YMCAs back home. Secretaries from Naismith's YMCA, which is now Springfield College, helped teach the game in New England. A national magazine article by Naismith described the sport and its rules for

In the 1890s the action stopped while the ball was retrieved from the basket. Games were often won by a team scoring 10 points or less.

the entire nation. But the game still had no name. One of the students, Frank Mahan, suggested it be called "Naismith ball." The humble Naismith dismissed the thought, so Mahan said, "Why not call it basket ball?"

In the beginning, there wasn't a limit to the number of players. Sometimes as many as 80 crowded the floor. Naismith thought 18 was about right, but by the turn of the century, he realized that five on a team seemed the best number for a game of three 20-minute periods.

Early basketball courts varied in size because gyms were not standard. Games were played in armories, dance halls, and skating rinks. Some courts had huge support posts in the middle of the floor. This led to the creation of the "post play," in which an offensive player drove the defender into the post, a play still used with individual players acting as the post to screen off a defender.

Girls have been playing basketball since the sport was invented in 1891.

Sometimes they played with an oval-shaped rugby ball, which was nearly impossible to dribble. By 1895, a standard ball and goal were adopted. The ball was four inches in diameter bigger than a soccer ball, slightly larger than the modern basketball. Made of four pieces of leather sewn together with thick laces, the ball was hard to handle and didn't last long. A shot off the backboard might hit on the laces, sending the ball bouncing in unpredictable directions.

Soft wire backboards were invented to keep the spectators from leaning over the balcony and blocking the ball from the basket. But the backboards would become so dented, it was impossible to get a shot to bank into the basket. Wooden backboards gradually replaced the wire. In some places the basket hung from the top of a pole without a backboard.

The early peach baskets gave way to a metal basket from which the ball had to be pushed out with a pole. In the mid-1890s, a Rhode Island company manufactured an 18-inch iron hoop with a cord net. Each goal had a long cord; when a basket was scored, the referee pulled the cord, lifting the net and popping the ball over the top of the hoop. Each score was followed by a jump ball in the center of the court, which greatly slowed the pace of the game. After 1937, the ball automatically went to the team that had been scored upon, leading to a faster-paced game.

In the beginning, field goals counted for one point, and a player who fouled was sent to a penalty box, as in ice hockey. If a team fouled three consecutive times, the opponent got a field goal. That rule was eventually replaced by free throws.

Dr. James Naismith, inventor of basketball, studied medicine and became a minister. In 1899 he went to the University of Kansas, where he coached the school team for 10 years. He would often watch his sport in amazement and marvel at how the game was growing.

By 1895, field goals were worth two points and free throws one. For many years, each team had one player who shot all the free throws. This rule was created to prevent a team from constantly fouling the worst shooter. In 1910, a New York league changed the rule to require the man who was fouled to shoot the free throw. Other leagues soon adopted it.

Strategies were very basic for a slow game that emphasized defense. Twenty points was usually enough to win a game. The defense was man-to-man and very physical. Players stood flatfooted and shot with two hands. The dribble was created as an escape from the defense. Players could dribble with both hands, which would be a violation under modern rules. They could also run down the court, tapping the ball in the air without it touching the floor. Until 1916, a player could not shoot after dribbling. He had to pass the ball.

When a ball went out of bounds, the team that got to the ball first gained possession. This caused teams to go crashing into the spectators, hoping to grab the ball. In one game, the ball rolled into a stairway. The players from one team crowded after it, so two opposing players lifted one of their mates to the edge of the balcony. From there, he swung over the bundled opponents, jumped into the stairway, and retrieved the ball.

The participation in basketball grew until more than 250 million people played it in some organized version, making it the most popular sport in the world. The game's rules have been translated into more than 30 languages. A handful of players and teams were responsible for much of the growth of the game's popularity.

ORIGINAL THIRTEEN RULES OF "BASKET BALL"

Dr. James Naismith drafted the following rules of basket ball and posted them before class in the gymnasium of the International YMCA Training School in Springfield, Massachusetts, on December 21, 1891:

1. The ball may be thrown in any direction with one and/or both hands.

2. The ball may be batted in any direction with one hand or both hands (but never the fist).

3. A player cannot run with the ball, the player must throw it from the spot on which he catches it, allowance to be made for a man who catches the ball when running at good speed.

4. The ball must be held in or between the hands; the arms or body must not be used for holding it.

5. No shouldering, holding, pushing, tripping or striking in any way the person of an opponent shall be allowed. The first infringement of this rule by any person shall count as a foul, the second shall disqualify him until the next goal is made, or if there was evident intent to injure the person, for the whole of the game, no substitute allowed.

6. A foul is striking the ball with the fist, violation of rules 3 and 4, and described in rule 5.

7. If either side makes three consecutive fouls it shall count a goal for the opponents (consecutive means without the opponents in the meantime making a foul).

8. A goal shall be made when the ball is thrown or batted from the grounds into the basket and stays there, providing those defending the goal do not touch or disturb the goal. If the ball rests on the edge and the opponent moves the basket it shall count as a goal.

9. When the ball goes out of bounds it shall be thrown into the field, and played by the person first touching it. In case of a dispute the umpire shall throw it straight into the field. The thrower is allowed five seconds, if he holds it longer it shall go to the opponent. If any side persists in delaying the game, the umpire shall call a foul on them.

10. The umpire shall be the judge of the men, and shall note the fouls, and notify the referee when three consecutive fouls have been made. He shall have power to disqualify men according to rule 5.

11. The referee shall be the judge of the ball and shall decide when the ball is in play, in bounds, and to which side it belongs, and shall keep the time. He shall decide when a goal has been made, and keep account of the goals with any other duties that are usually performed by a referee.

12. The time shall be two fifteen minute halves, with five minutes rest between.

13. The side making the most goals in that time shall be declared the winner. In case of a draw the game may, by agreement of the captains, be continued until another goal is made.

3

THE EARLY PROFESSIONALS

The popularity of professional baseball in the 1890s helped pro basketball take root. The first all-professional basketball team played in Trenton, New Jersey, in 1896. They opened the season by beating the Brooklyn YMCA, 16–1, on Saturday, November 7, in front of 700 curious onlookers. Each player received about $15.

The court at that first game had a 12-foot fence around the sidelines to keep the ball—and pursuing players—from going into the crowd. Many gyms built cages around their court so the game would move faster and there would be fewer fights for loose balls—thus the nickname of "cagers" for basketball players was born.

By the late 1890s, many professional teams flourished in the Northeast. Teams in New Jersey and Philadelphia formed the first pro league, the National Basketball League, in 1898. Players earned $2.50 for home games and $1.25 for road games. Trenton won the first two championships in a 20-game schedule.

The National League lasted five years while other leagues came and went. Many teams hired players on a per-game basis; a player could earn a living by playing six nights a week. By 1915, some were earning $7,500 a year as full-time basketball players.

Many local leagues and traveling independent teams sprang up around that time. The first great professional team was the Buffalo Germans. Formed in 1895 and consisting of 14-year-old

The Harlem Globetrotters have been entertaining audiences all over the world for more than 70 years with their combination of clowning and skillful basketball.

19

YMCA students, they became so good that they commanded as much as $5,000 for a three-game series. They had an 111-game winning streak, and over 20 years posted a 792–86 record.

The traveling Celtics of New York, sometimes called the Original Celtics, dominated the 1920s. In 1922–23, they barnstormed across the country, winning 193 and losing 11. They drew huge crowds and earned large salaries. The roster included Horse Haggerty at center; Johnny Beckman, the "Babe Ruth of Basketball," and Nat Holman, the best scorer and passer in the country, at forwards; Dutch Dehnert and Chris Leonard, guards; and Pete Barry, Johnny Whitty, and Joe Lapchick off the bench. They played a quick and structured kind of basketball unlike anyone else, perfecting the give-and-go play, the pivot in the middle, switching on defense, and passing to the open man.

The Original Celtics played more than 150 games a year and won 90 percent of them. When the American Basketball League organized in 1925, the Celtics refused to join. But the next year, when the Brooklyn team folded, the Celtics replaced them and won the championship with ease. The Celtics' dominance of the league and the rough play turned fans off the game. The constant fouling and wrestling matches on the floor forced the league to draft a new rule that disqualified players if they picked up five fouls. But it was not enough to save the league, which closed in 1931.

The Original Celtics reorganized, but they were no longer the best team in New York. From 1932 to 1936, the all-black New York Rens won 473 and lost 49, including an 88-game winning streak. Guard Fats Jenkins was the captain and star. Eyre Saitch was one of the best long shooters in the country. Center Tarzan Cooper became a master of the pivot play.

The Rens won 112 and lost 7 in 1939 and captured the pro world championship. But they were soon overtaken in skill and popularity by the Harlem Globetrotters. Formed by Abe Saperstein in 1927, the all-black Globetrotters were almost unbeatable. Like the Rens, they suffered the pitfalls of black teams of the time. They were not allowed to join white leagues. Some states had laws that prohibited blacks from competing against whites. The Globetrotters and Rens found it difficult to get food

The New York Rens were basketball's best independent team in the 1930s. They barnstormed around the country playing more than 100 games a year.

THE RENAISSANCE, THE GREATEST COLORED BASKETBALL TEAM OF ALL-TIME

Left to right: Clarence "Fat" Jenkins, Bill Yancey, John Holt, James "Pappy" Ricks, Eyre Saitch, Charles "Tarzan" Cooper and "Wee Willie" Smith. Inset: Owner Robert L. Douglas, who organized club in 1922-23.

and lodging on the road. In some of the cities they visited, white kids had never seen blacks. They would rub the players' skin to see if the color came off.

The Globetrotters believed that basketball should be entertaining, but they also played well, winning the 1940 world championship. They trotted around the globe, electrifying crowds as large as the 75,000 who watched them in Berlin in 1951 with their fast-paced game, fancy ball handling, and showmanship. Louis "Babe" Pressley could throw a pass with so much backspin that it would bounce right back to him, as if on a string. Inman Jackson would roll the ball up one arm, across his

Reece "Goose" Tatum was a leading actor, juggler, and playmaker for the Harlem Globetrotters in the 1940s and '50s.

shoulders, and down the other arm. Goose Tatum would spin the ball on his fingertip.

Sometimes Tatum would fall to the floor while taking a shot, acting as if he'd been knocked unconscious. While worried teammates huddled around him, someone would remove one of his sneakers and hold it under Tatum's nose. Suddenly, Tatum would leap to his feet with his eyes bobbing and his nose twitching. The crowds loved it.

When the National Basketball League, forerunner of the NBA, organized in 1937, many of the best college players signed. Barnstorming teams like the Rens gradually faded away, although the Globetrotters remained in business. But the Original Celtics, the Rens, and the Globetrotters had a permanent impact on the game. Fast-paced action, ball handling, set plays, and showmanship—all elements they introduced—became the foundations of the pro game that followed.

THE FIRST BIG MEN

As a tall, clumsy boy wearing glasses, George Mikan was so filled with bitterness, he said, "My height nearly wrecked my life." By the time he was 18, he was 6' 10" and weighed 245 pounds. Mikan was born in Joliet, Illinois, in 1924, a time when few people reached 6 feet in height. Houses, beds, and other furniture were built for average-sized people. It was an uncomfortable world for Mikan.

In high school, his height attracted the basketball coach's attention. But a badly broken leg kept him off his feet for 18 months, setting back his chances to improve his athletic skills. Mikan was too uncoordinated to make the team.

Determined to play basketball, Mikan applied to Notre Dame. The coach rejected him because he was so awkward, adding, "Besides, he wears glasses."

Mikan enrolled at DePaul University in Chicago, where the coach, Ray Meyer, also thought he was hopeless on the court. Undaunted, Mikan designed his own training program. He skipped rope, shadow boxed, and played one-on-one games with the quickest guards at DePaul. Impressed by his attitude, Meyer began to work with him, developing accurate hook shots with either hand, and instilling in Mikan the confidence that his height was an advantage and not a handicap. Mikan became a three-time All-American and led DePaul to the NIT championship in 1945.

The first of the big men, 6' 10" George Mikan led his teams to six championships in seven years. Named by the Associated Press as the best player of the first half-century, Mikan was so dominant he caused the foul line to be widened from 6 to 12 feet.

When Mikan scored a phenomenal 53 points in the NIT semifinals—a total unheard of in 1945—he convinced the pros that a winning team could be built around a big man instead of relying on quickness. Mikan became pro basketball's first great center, dominating the game inside on offense and preventing scoring on defense. When double-teamed, he was an accurate passer, but his best weapon was his deadly hook shot. He also scored often by blocking out the defense and tapping in rebounds. Because of him, the lane was widened from six feet to 12 feet.

Signed out of college by the Chicago American Gears of the National Basketball League for $12,000, he led them to the title in 1947 by averaging 16.5 points and 19.7 rebounds a game. Mikan drew huge crowds, and the owners of arenas noticed. Looking for a way to fill their buildings during the winter, when circuses and rodeos were idle, they formed a new Basketball Association of America, which included the New York Knickerbockers, Philadelphia Warriors, Boston Celtics, and Chicago Stags (now Bulls).

Mikan's Chicago team folded in 1947, and he was assigned to a new team, the Minneapolis Lakers. Two years later, the NBL and BAA merged, forming the 17-team National Basketball Association. With Mikan, Alex Groza of Indianapolis, and St. Louis's Ed Macauley, the NBA featured high-scoring players and quick offenses. Fans flocked to see Mikan, who led the new league in scoring for its first three years. The Lakers won three championships in four years. After beating the Knicks for the Lakers' third in a row in 1953, Mikan and his sore knees decided it was time to retire.

The next generation of big men was not far off. Bill Russell, a 6' 10" defensive specialist, had idolized Mikan as a boy. Russell led the University of San Francisco to two NCAA titles and a 55-game winning streak. The Boston Celtics signed him in 1956, and he helped them win their first title with his shot-blocking, rebounding, and all-around defensive play.

The key to the Celtics' glory under coach Red Auerbach was Russell. The fabled Celtics fast break usually consisted of a Russell rebound or blocked shot, an outlet pass to ball-handling wizard Bob Cousy, and a goal by Bill Sharman, the league's best shooter, or Tom Heinsohn. Russell's long, spindly arms made shooters change the arc on their shot.

The Boston Celtics' coach for 16 years and general manager for 34, Arnold "Red" Auerbach brought 16 NBA titles to Boston Garden, relying on a strong defense and running game. Here he talks to his team during a timeout. "Strategy is something anyone can learn," he said about coaching, "but not all coaches take time to understand a man's personality."

Bill Russell led the University of San Francisco to 55 straight wins and two NCAA championships with his shot-blocking and rebounding skills before winning nine NBA titles in 10 years with the Celtics. He was a five-time MVP.

No one in history was a better rebounder. As a rookie in 1957, he had 32 rebounds in Boston's 125–123 double-overtime loss to St. Louis for the NBA title. The age of the rebounder was born. In the playoffs, he averaged almost 25 per game. On offense, he averaged 15 points over his career.

Russell was the first great player at blocking out an opponent. Bob Pettit, Wes Unseld, Paul Silas, Moses Malone, Charles Barkley, and Dennis Rodman would later emulate Russell's aggressiveness on the boards—a skill that helped the Celtics win 11 championships from 1956 through '69. Nine of those titles came under Auerbach, who was replaced by Russell in 1967. By that time, Russell had lost the spotlight to the newest big man, Wilt the Stilt.

Born in Philadelphia in 1936, Wilt Chamberlain was already 6' 11" when he entered high school. By the time he chose the University of Kansas out of more than 200 colleges pursuing him, he had grown to 7' 2" and 275 pounds. At Kansas he scored 52 points in his first game. Hastily adapted swarming defenses "held" him to just under 30 points a game for the next three years.

Chamberlain traveled with the Harlem Globetrotters for a year before signing with the Philadelphia Warriors in 1959. No player has had such an immediate impact on the league as Chamberlain. He averaged 38.4 points and 27.2 rebounds a game as a rookie.

Chamberlain etched his name in history in 1962, when he scored a record 100 points in a 169–147 win against the Knicks. Chamberlain was on a mission that night. All season he had been breaking pro basketball scoring records, having hit a high of 78 points one night. He averaged 50 points a game for the season, and his 42 points in the All-Star Game remained a record more than 30 years later.

But against the Knicks on March 2, it soon became evident that he would shatter his own single-game scoring record. At the end of three quarters, he had 69 points. The crowd,

Two stars go up against each other as Bill Russell tries to block Wilt Chamberlain in a 1962 Celtics vs. Warriors game. Both players were selected to the NBA's all-time team.

realizing they might see history, stood and cheered for him as the fourth quarter started. They hoped they might even see a player reach 100 points in a game.

The Knicks realized that possibility, too, but they took a different view, especially after Chamberlain scored his 79th point.

"The Knicks decided they didn't want someone to score 100 points against them," Chamberlain recalled. "They started to do anything they could to prevent me from getting 100 points. They'd foul my teammates intentionally so the ball wouldn't come to me. But they couldn't get the ball from Guy Rodgers, he was so fast. They couldn't even foul him. And when the ball got to me, they'd foul me immediately. They wouldn't even try to stop me. Just foul me and hope I missed the foul shots.

"When I realized they didn't want me to score 100, that served as my motivation."

His total reached 98 with about a minute to play. After an exchange of possessions, Ted Luckenbill fed Chamberlain the ball in the pivot. He missed the shot, grabbed the rebound, and missed again. Luckenbill scrambled for the ball and passed it to Joe Ruklick, who tossed a high pass above the rim. This time, with 46 seconds left to play, Chamberlain grabbed the ball and stuffed it through the basket for his 100th point. He had hit 36 of 63 from the floor and 28 of 32 free-throw attempts.

Despite averaging a record 50.4 points a game and having the greatest season in history, the year ended bitterly for Chamberlain. The Warriors lost the Eastern Conference championship to the Celtics in a 109–107 Game 7 defeat.

THE FIRST BIG MEN ♦ 31

For the next five years, Chamberlain's teams lost to the Celtics in the playoffs. The Warriors moved to San Francisco at the start of the 1962–63 season and traded Chamberlain to the new Philadelphia 76ers in 1964. In 1967 Chamberlain finally prevailed over the Celtics, the 76ers defeating the eight-time defending champs, 4 games to 1. Chamberlain had 41 rebounds in one of the games. Then they defeated the Warriors in the finals, and Chamberlain at last had his championship. The next season he stepped up his passing game to thwart double-teaming defenses and became the only center ever to lead the NBA in assists.

Traded to the Lakers in 1969, Chamberlain won his second championship with them in 1972, then retired as the league's first 30,000-point scorer. Chamberlain also held the record for rebounds, snaring 55 against Boston one night in 1960, and finished with almost 24,000 rebounds in his career.

No big man had ever dominated the game like Wilt Chamberlain. On his tall shoulders, and those of George Mikan and Bill Russell, the NBA grew.

5 THE WAKE-UP CALL

When George Mikan retired after the 1954 season, pro basketball had a problem. Games had become pushing and shoving matches inside the lane. Officials tried to maintain order by calling more fouls, but watching teams shoot 30 free throws a game put fans to sleep. The action also dragged when a team leading in the fourth quarter ran out the clock by stalling on offense, freezing the ball.

Those conditions inspired the two most significant basketball rules changes in history. First the league cut down on intentional fouling by limiting teams to five fouls per period. After five, the opponent would receive a penalty free throw. To avoid the slowdowns in the action, the NBA then created the 24-second shot clock. Scores jumped from 79.5 per game in 1953–54 to 93 points per game in 1954–55. The Celtics averaged more than 101. Suddenly, fast breaks became more common, and the speed and skill of the players could be more fully displayed. Shooters such as Dolph Schayes, Paul Arizin, and Bob Pettit thrived under the new rules. The Celtics, with ball-handling wizard Bob Cousy as their playmaker, built their dynasty around speed, defense, and the fast break.

Cousy popularized dribbling and ballhandling. He was considered a magician for the way he could suddenly disappear from a defender's sight—dribbling behind the back and darting around him. He ran the floor as if the ball was

Ball-handling wizard Bob Cousy was the playmaker of the Celtics' champions in the 1950s and '60s. He set an NBA record with 28 assists in one game in 1959.

an attachment to his hand, yo-yoing on a string while he was in full sprint.

The Celtics' excellence and the presence of Wilt Chamberlain kept the NBA in the winter sports spotlight. But the game was still basically glued to the floor. The stars played with skill and precision, but with few acrobatics. Many teams were in financial trouble. Pro basketball still lagged behind baseball and football in popularity.

Sensing a market for a more dynamic game, promoters formed the rival American Basketball League in 1961. The league lasted only two seasons, but it left two legacies: the first black coach of a major professional team, John McLendon of the Cleveland Pipers, and the three-point shot.

A better-financed group of backers formed the American Basketball Association in 1967. The ABA began without a TV deal or a big-name player. That soon changed. The ABA lured away NBA stars with salaries topping $200,000. NBA scoring champ Rick Barry of the Warriors was the first to jump, and others soon followed. Denver signed University of Detroit center Spencer Heywood, the first player to leave college early and be allowed to play professionally. By 1970 the two leagues were in an all-out war for players and fans.

Aside from money, the ABA offered something the NBA lacked: style and color. The ABA used a red, white, and blue ball that one NBA coach said "belongs on the nose of a seal." The ABA adopted the three-point shot and promoted a flamboyant style of play that featured high jumps and power dunks, small, quick guards, a running game, and trapping defenses. For most of its history, the NBA had regarded the dunk as a hot dog play. The ABA made it a signature of the new era of the game.

The dunk was made famous by Oklahoma A&M's Bob Kurland, who used the play to help the Aggies win the 1945 NCAA championship. It was not a common offensive weapon at the time. College basketball even outlawed it from 1967–76.

The Baltimore Bullets' Gus Johnson was the first NBA player to use what playground players might call "punk dunk," or "in-your-face" dunking. Johnson's dunks were so forceful that he broke three backboards in his career. Whenever he dunked at home as a rookie in 1963, the sound of a gunshot went off over the loud speakers. "When I dunked that ball and heard that shot for the first time, I said to myself, 'Uh-oh, Gus. Somebody done gotcha.' "

The 76ers' Darryl Dawkins broke two back-boards in less than a month in 1979. The first incident brought a rain of glass on Bill Robinzine of the Kansas City Kings, so the colorful Dawkins dubbed the monster jam the "chocolate-thunder flyin', Robinzine-cryin', teeth-shakin', glass-breakin', rump-roastin', bun-toasting, wham, bam, glass-breaker-I-am jam." Dawkins' jams led to the invention of the collapsible rim.

Long before the modern dunking stars such as Michael Jordan, Grant Hill, Shaquille O'Neal, and even Spud Webb, who at 5' 7" won the 1986 slam-dunk contest at the All-Star Game, the players in the ABA brought the art of the dunk to the game.

Connie Hawkins led the Pittsburgh Pipers to the first ABA championship with his high-flying, windmill jams—a sight never seen in colleges or the pros. Darnell Hillman of the Indiana Pacers could jump so high that he once won a bet by leaping to the top of the backboard to fetch a $10 bill. San Antonio's George Gervin made up his dunks in mid-air. He would fly past the goal and then reach back and slam the ball as he passed by.

But the master was Julius Erving.

The struggling ABA survived having 28 different franchises in nine years in great part because of Dr. J. The Virginia Squires signed him after his second year at the University of Massachusetts in 1971. The financially strapped Squires later traded him to the New York Nets, who won ABA titles with Erving in 1974 and '76.

Erving literally brought pro basketball to a higher level. With his outstanding jumping ability and balance, he made drives to the basket that no one had ever seen. One of his favorite moves was getting a running start on the baseline and jumping up to dunk. But at the last second, he would duck underneath the goal and reverse slam without turning to look at the basket.

Erving's most famous move came at the 1976 ABA All-Star Game in Denver. In the first known dunking contest, he ran the length of the floor, leaped at the foul line, and seemed to float like a feather through the air, whirling the ball in his right hand and slamming it through the net. The crowd and players went crazy, and a national TV audience gasped in awe.

The presence of Erving and the wide-open style of play helped the ABA lure some of the best young players, including Gervin, Artis Gilmore, Dan Issel, Moses Malone, David

*The Philadelphia 76ers'
Julius Erving flies through
the air over Larry Bird
en route to a slam dunk
in a 1982 playoff game.
The 6' 6" Dr. J brought
the high-altitude game
to the NBA and was the
third pro player to score
30,000 points, after Wilt
Chamberlain and Kareem
Abdul-Jabbar.*

Thompson, and George McGinnis. But the ABA
never got the big TV contract it needed. By 1976
it had accumulated $50 million in debts.

After a series of legal battles over player
rights, the ABA and NBA agreed to merge. The
NBA took in four teams—the New Jersey
Nets, Denver Nuggets, San Antonio Spurs, and

Indiana Pacers. The Nets sold Erving to the Philadelphia 76ers for $3 million to help pay the fee for entering the NBA.

The veteran players of the NBA resented the new teams and players, but the infusion of ABA talent saved the NBA.

In the first year after the merger, Denver won the Midwest Division. Four of the top 10 scorers, five of the 10 starters in the NBA finals between Portland and Philadelphia, and 10 of the 24 All-Stars were ABA alumni. Moses Malone was the league's best rebounder, George Gervin the best scorer, and Dr. J the top attraction.

"Listen, the ABA gave the NBA a wakeup call," Erving said. "We were the first league that really knew how to promote its teams and its stars. What the NBA does now with Michael Jordan . . . the ABA was doing with players such as George McGinnis, George Gervin, and myself. In my mind, the NBA has just become a bigger version of the ABA. They play the style of game that we did. They sell their stars like we did. The only difference is that they have more resources and can do it on a much grander scale that we in the ABA ever could."

A year later, in 1978–79, the NBA had a different kind of problem. Early in the season, Lakers center Kareem Abdul-Jabbar broke his hand when he punched Milwaukee's Kent Benson. A few weeks later, the Lakers' Kermit Washington slugged Houston's Rudy Tomjanovich in the face, crushing his cheekbone and nearly killing him. Defending champion Portland lost their star center, Bill Walton, to a foot injury two-thirds of the way through the year. Rumors of widespread drug use by players rocked the league. Television ratings plummeted.

Players were called outlaws, thugs and drug addicts.

The NBA lacked a great team and fresh young stars to draw attention away from their problems. Then, in 1979, the basketball gods granted the league what it needed: Larry Bird and Magic Johnson arrived.

6 THE MODERN STARS

When Larry Bird and Earvin "Magic" Johnson entered the NBA in 1979, fan interest in the game was at a low level. The league had not introduced an exciting rookie since Bill Walton in 1974. Other than Julius Erving, their only true superstars were Pete Maravich and Kareem Abdul-Jabbar.

Born Lew Alcindor in New York City in 1947, the 7' 2", 235-pound Abdul-Jabbar led UCLA to three straight NCAA championships. He signed a million-dollar contract with the Milwaukee Bucks in 1969 and later changed his name to the Muslim Kareem Abdul-Jabbar.

A six-time MVP with the Bucks and Los Angeles Lakers, Kareem played on six NBA champions. He could do it all: score, pass, rebound, block shots, play defense. He scored on dunks, fadeaways, short jumpers, finger rolls, and one-handers. He perfected the sky hook, launching it with either hand—the ball rising so high at the point of release that no one could block it. His coach with the Lakers, Pat Riley, called the skyhook "the most awesome weapon in the history of any sport."

By the time he retired in 1989, Abdul-Jabbar was the all-time leader in 20 categories.

Kareem's dominance in the middle continued the trend of building winning teams around big men. But as the NBA entered the 1980s, there were not many good big men coming into the

Magic Johnson fools Isiah Thomas (left) and Julius Erving by passing off instead of going to the hoop during the 1985 All-Star Game. As adept at steals as assists and scoring, Johnson played on five NBA champions and was the playoff MVP three times.

league. So the game became quicker, with faster guards, agile forwards, and better passing.

There has never been a better ball handler than Maravich, who was called "Pistol Pete" because he wasn't shy about firing a shot. As a boy, he would sit in the aisle seat at the movies so he could practice his dribbling in the dark. He rarely went anywhere without a ball in his hand. He dribbled between his legs, behind his back, and in a low, pushing, close-to-the-ground motion. As a 10th-grader in high school, he once threw a behind-the-back bounce pass through an opponent's legs to a teammate, who made a layup on the assist. Maravich was so dazzling that his first NBA team, the Atlanta Hawks, often asked him to put on dribbling shows for fans at halftime. He would spin balls on his fingertips, through his legs, and make no-look passes to one direction while faking a pass with the other hand.

Passing and scoring were the qualities in which Magic Johnson and Larry Bird excelled. They first faced each other in the 1979 NCAA championship, where Johnson's Michigan State Spartans defeated Bird's undefeated and top-ranked Indiana State Sycamores. Magic and Bird then signed with the most storied franchises: Bird with the Celtics and Johnson with the Lakers. The Celtics won three and the Lakers five of the next 10 NBA championships. Three times the rivals met in the finals.

At 6' 9", Johnson was the tallest point guard in history. He was so athletic he could have played any position, and his speed and dazzling passes led the "Showtime" Lakers of the 1980s to five NBA championships. Magic made the triple-double of at least 10 points, rebounds, and assists per game a common statistic. Often he would grab a rebound, run the length of the court, and find an open man with a no-look pass or 20-foot bounce across the lane. On the fast break, he invented ways to score. His instinct told him to get a teammate the good shot. If the fast break failed, he would drop in a long-range jumper.

Magic's signature was his passing. Where Bob Cousy, Hot Rod Hundley, and Pete Maravich had perfected weaving, on-the-run, behind-the-back styles, Magic would not only throw behind the back, but without looking. He had an uncanny ability to make the right pass—with the exact touch—at the perfect moment.

Magic was All-NBA nine times and regular-season and playoff MVP three times. Perhaps his greatest moment came in his rookie season. Abdul-Jabbar scored 40 points in Game 5 of the 1980 finals to give the Lakers a 3–2 lead against Seattle, But he badly sprained his ankle, so Johnson had to replace him at center in Game 6. Magic scored 42 points and had 15 rebounds to clinch the Lakers' first championship since 1972.

Johnson retired abruptly in 1991 when he announced that he had contracted the virus that causes AIDS. He attempted two comebacks, but left the NBA for good in 1996. Always a promoter of basketball and popular with fans because of his wide, easy smile, Magic brought American basketball to many countries in the world by playing in exhibition games.

Larry Bird and Magic were good friends, but their personalities were opposites. The shy, 6' 9" Bird came from a small town, French

Lick, Indiana. One of the best shooters in history, he could hit the long jumper with a defender right in his face. After regular practice, he would remain alone for hours practicing his shooting—especially without looking at the basket. He learned to feel for how long a shot needed to be. He shot layups and short jumpers with either hand, ventured beyond the three-point line, and shot from all angles.

Bird's scoring ability helped bring a lost art back to the game—shooting. Offenses had become sluggish and too dependent on dunks. Bird was not conventional. He was a throwback.

Originally, players shot two-handed and even under-handed. Hank Luisetti of Stanford had introduced the one-handed shot in the mid-1930s. Wyoming's Kenny Sailors made the jump shot popular in 1940. By 1958, players such as Paul Arizin of the Warriors were releasing the ball farther behind their head to keep defenses from blocking their shots. Along the way, Jerry West of the Lakers became an excellent jump shooter, especially with the game on the line. In many ways, Larry Bird reminded a lot of people of West.

Dubbed "Larry Legend," Bird had a penchant for the dramatic. In Game 2 of the 1984 finals against the Lakers, the Celtics' offense began to unravel. Coach K. C. Jones called a time-out. In the huddle, Bird grabbed Jones and said, "K. C., give me the ball. I know what to do."

"Shut up, Larry. I'm the coach of this team," Jones snapped.

Jones then turned to his team and said, "Here's what I want. Inbound the ball, get it to Larry, and everybody else get out of the way."

An all-NBA forward nine times, Larry Bird could score from inside or outside, was deadly accurate at the free throw line, and was an outstanding passer for the Boston Celtics from 1979 to 1992. Here he drives around Kareem Abdul-Jabbar of the Lakers in the 1987 playoffs.

Bird scored after the time-out, leading the Celtics to victory that day and to the championship in seven games.

In Game 5 of the 1987 Eastern Conference finals against Detroit, the Celtics trailed by one point with five seconds to play. The series was tied 2–2. Standing on the sideline, Pistons guard Isiah Thomas prepared to inbound the ball. He threw. Bird spun around, stole the pass, and flipped it to Dennis Johnson for a layup that won the game.

Larry Legend was always confident. At the 1986 All-Star Game three-point shooting contest, he lined up with the eight other contestants and said, "Which one of you guys is going to finish second?"

His place in history assured, Bird retired in 1992 after 13 seasons because of an ailing back.

A new breed of centers finally came along in the 1980s. Among the best of the cat-quick, 7-foot centers was Hakeem Olajuwon of the Houston Rockets. Taken with the first pick of the 1984 draft, Olajuwon became an immediate force. He blocked shots, scored inside and out, rebounded, and ran the floor, often grabbing the rebound, rushing downcourt, and finishing off the play with a power move to the basket.

Olajuwon, who played soccer as a child growing up in Nigeria, led the Rockets to back-to-back championships in 1994 and '95 and was the league's MVP in 1994. His closest rival was Patrick Ewing of the Knicks, another quick and dominating defensive player.

By the time the Knicks became competitive, however, the Pistons were replacing the Celtics as the best team in the East. In 1989–90, the Pistons became the sixth team to win back-to-back titles. They intimidated and outran opponents behind the brilliant playmaking of Isiah Thomas, the rebounding of Dennis Rodman, the muscle of Bill Laimbeer, and the leadership and clutch scoring of Joe Dumars.

Michael Jordan and the Chicago Bulls dominated the NBA in the 1990s. Excelling in every phase of the game, Jordan was a born winner. He capped his freshman year at the

University of North Carolina by hitting the winning shot in the Tar Heels' 63–62 win against Georgetown for the 1982 NCAA championship. He led the U.S. Olympic team to a gold medal before joining the Bulls in 1984.

The 6' 6", 198-pound guard could lead the NBA in scoring or steals, once doing both in the same season. He was the MVP and the defensive player of the year in 1988. The Bulls won three NBA titles in a row through 1993; Jordan was the playoffs' MVP each year.

But Jordan was more than just a great player. His exuberant style on the court and outgoing personality gave the NBA a much-needed promotional focus. Michael was marketable. He earned $50 million a year from endorsements and became the best known athlete in the world.

Everybody wanted to be like Mike. For years basketball shorts had been cut short and tight-fitting. Jordan liked his long and baggy. Soon the whole league—and leisure shorts, in general—followed that style. Jordan wore his socks low, so the decades-old style of long tube socks to the knees quickly disappeared.

A 1994 medical report revealed that emergency rooms were treating an abnormal number of severe tongue bites among children. Apparently, kids playing hoops had been imitating Jordan's tongue-waggling as he drove to the basket.

Then, citing mental fatigue and the anguish over the murder of his father in the summer of 1993, Michael Jordan abruptly retired after just nine seasons. The NBA's marquee stars—Julius Erving, Larry Bird, Magic Johnson, Michael Jordan—were all

While NBA stars had the most visibility, the spread of basketball's popularity around the world was evident by American servicemen playing pick-up games wherever they were stationed, even on an aircraft carrier at sea.

gone. There were good young players coming along, but none was a Michael Jordan, on or off the court. In Jordan's absence, the NBA endured some of its worst publicity since the late 1970s. Players such as Derrick Coleman, Nick Van Exel, and Dennis Rodman were called thugs, malcontents, and troublemakers. Van Exel hit a referee and defied his coaches. Rodman had a habit of being thrown out of games and outraging fans and teammates with his actions on and off the court.

Then, after his unsuccessful attempt to become a pro baseball player, Michael Jordan returned to basketball.

Older, wiser, and a different player, the new Jordan led the Bulls to NBA titles in 1996 and '97 as effectively as the old Jordan had done.

"Now I'm into doing things that lead to a win, and I also have more weapons to work with," he said. "I'm a better passer, a better shooter. I have better range. I can shoot the three. So I don't have to dunk as much now, especially when the dunk isn't there. I'm not going to force it and take it to the hole against four or five guys. I'll pull up and take the J [jumper]."

"Hey, the man is still doing it," said Golden State guard Chris Mullin. "He's still the best, doing everything he's ever done and more. Maybe he's doing it a little differently, but he's still the best."

7

THE FUTURE

By the 1990s, the NBA had achieved world-wide popularity. The game was being played in Asia, Europe, Africa, and Central America. The league conducted clinics in foreign countries and actively scouted players abroad. When the Chicago Bulls won their fifth championship in seven years in 1997, the finals were seen in more than 400 million homes in 93 countries.

The use of pro players in the 1992 Olympics for the first time gave the game a boost. The "Dream Team" of Magic Johnson, Larry Bird, David Robinson, Charles Barkley, Michael Jordan, Chris Mullin, Scottie Pippen, Patrick Ewing, Christian Laetner, Karl Malone, and John Stockton took the gold medal with ease as millions watched around the world.

The NBA had become the model sports league under the leadership of commissioner David Stern. Its international outlook led to consideration of a World Cup tournament similar to soccer's quadrennial event. Stern's promotional skills and the league's expansion helped NBA attendance rise 42 percent in the late 1980s. Revenues of NBA-licensed items climbed to $125 million a year.

When fans voted on the NBA's 50 greatest players for its golden anniversary celebration in 1996, they chose 11 active players along with the legendary Chamberlain, Russell, Abdul-Jabbar, Mikan, Robertson, Bird, and Magic

Orlando center Shaquille O'Neal blocks Karl Malone's approach to the basket during the 1997 All-Star Game. O'Neal was one of the NBA's most visible and popular stars as the 20th century ended.

Johnson. The inclusion of so many current players reflected in part the power of the NBA's marketing muscle. The league promoted players, not teams. Fans identified with Charles Barkley's growls, Shaquille O'Neal's monster dunks, and everything that Michael Jordan did.

"What you have in basketball that the other sports don't have," said associate editor Kurt Badenhausen of *Financial World* magazine, "is personalities like Shaq and Jordan and Dennis Rodman, who have the personality and drawing power to sell products and memorabilia. It's that simple."

A 1996 poll revealed that 45 percent of the respondents said their interest in basketball had grown in the early 1990s. As attendance continued to climb, the league led all sports in sales of merchandise, much of it in cooperation with corporate giants such as Nike, McDonald's, Disney, and AT&T.

New stars emerged. In the West, the Utah Jazz built a winning team around forward Karl "Mail Man" Malone and point guard John Stockton. Stockton had arrived from tiny Gonzaga College in 1984. The 6' 9" Malone had been one of the nation's leading scorers and rebounders at Louisiana Tech. The two teammates and best friends helped the Jazz become annual contenders for the Western Conference championship. Malone set a record by scoring at least 2,000 points for 10 straight years; Stockton became the NBA's all-time leader in steals and assists.

The power-dunking center Shaquille O'Neal came out of LSU to become a big favorite of young fans. Off the court, he was visible as a rap singer and movie star and on frequent television commercials. The first pick in the 1992 draft, O'Neal made the Orlando Magic an immediate contender before signing with the Los Angeles Lakers in 1996.

Penny Hardaway arrived from Memphis in 1994 and reminded observers of Magic Johnson. A smooth, slick passer who took charge on the court, Hardaway was quiet and shy. Raised by his grandmother in a poor section of Memphis, he had played basketball under street lights late into the night. With dedication and practice, he became an NBA star, averaging almost 20 points, 7 assists, and 5 rebounds.

Grant Hill joined the Detroit Pistons out of Duke University, which had won NCAA championships in his first two years. A brilliant front court player, Hill dazzled fans with his spinning moves and cat-quick drives to the

Grant Hill of the Detroit Pistons is fouled by the Heat's Alonzo Mourning. After starring at Duke, Hill became a favorite of NBA fans without the hype and controversy that surrounded some stars.

basket. A master of the triple-double, in 1996 he became the 15th player to lead his team in points, rebounds, and assists.

At a time when some players refused to practice and acted like spoiled brats, Hill was a breath of fresh air. He was polite, smart, and appreciative of being a professional athlete. His parents had raised him on the importance of education and kindness to others. He did not take his talent for granted, and was actually embarrassed when fans elected him as the first rookie to start in an NBA All-Star Game. Touted as the new Dr. J or the new Jordan, Hill downplayed the hype. Fans loved him more.

The league continued to expand. The Charlotte Hornets and Miami Heat began play in 1988; the Minnesota Timberwolves and Orlando Magic came in a year later. In only nine years, all four made the playoffs. In 1996 the NBA moved into Canada, placing teams in Vancouver and Toronto.

Expansion brought growth, but along with it came a problem: the need for more players. Young and unproven players dropped out of college in greater numbers than ever in pursuit of stardom and wealth in the pro game. Many did not make it. Scotty Thurman, whose last-minute heroics had helped Arkansas win the 1995 NCAA title, left school early that year to enter the NBA. But nobody drafted him. He spent the next two years in minor and European basketball leagues. Thurman's story was typical of many who found themselves chasing a dream that may never come true.

The NBA began to fill its rosters by looking abroad. The Chicago Bulls signed Tony Kukoc, an Olympic star for his native Yugoslavia.

Detlef Schrempf from Germany joined the Seattle Supersonics. A 7' 3" center from Lithuania, Arvydas Sabonis, wound up with the Portland Trailblazers.

By opening its doors to foreign players, the NBA became a bigger and quicker league. Suddenly, point guards were 6' 6" and the average NBA height was 6' 7". Dunking the ball, a phenomenon rarely seen before 1970, became so common that some coaches believed the basket should be raised from 10 feet to 12 feet high. Since the 1950s, the standard NBA court had been 94 feet long and 50 feet wide. But as the players grew in height and speed, the court seemed to get smaller and more crowded. Fouls increased and scoring declined as defenses became stronger. Some of the game's governors considered moving the three-point line farther from the basket to open the lane.

When James Naismith invented basketball, he envisioned it as a game for all ages and both sexes. Women had played basketball from its beginnings, but nobody paid much attention to the girls' games until the 1970s, when women's college teams began to get newspaper and television coverage. As outstanding women such as Nancy Lieberman, Cheryl Miller, Ann Meyers, Lynette Woodard, Ann Donovan, and Carol Blazejowski earned more recognition, the women's teams attracted bigger followings.

But there was no professional league open to women. Only one, Lynette Woodard, had ever signed a pro contract. A four-time All-American at the University of Kansas, Woodard set the women's scoring record with 3,649 points. The gifted ball-handler played for the gold-medal

*Rebecca Lobo, 6' 4"
forward for the New York
Liberty in the Women's
NBA, played in 102
consecutive games without
a loss, spanning her senior
year at the University
of Connecticut, the U.S.
National team, the Olympics,
and the first seven games
of the WNBA's first season
in 1997.*

women's Olympic team in 1984, and in 1985
became the first woman to play for the Harlem
Globetrotters.

A few women's professional leagues started
up, but they all failed. When the 1994–95
University of Connecticut women capped a 35–0

season with the national title, the headlines and television exposure renewed interest in a women's league. The thrilling gold-medal performance of the U.S. women's team at the 1996 Olympics boosted that interest. Two professional leagues started up in 1997, the American Basketball League and the Women's National Basketball Association, which was sponsored by the NBA. Armed with a national TV contract and the marketing know-how of the NBA, the WNBA launched its summer schedule with eight teams: Cleveland, New York, Charlotte, and Houston in the Eastern Conference; Los Angeles, Phoenix, Sacramento, and Utah in the Western.

Some of the women had waited more than 10 years since their college days for a chance to earn a living as a pro. The oldest, Nancy Lieberman-Cline, was 38 when the WNBA season started.

The women's leagues were as international as the men's. Players on the opening rosters came from China, Italy, Japan, Russia, Brazil, Australia, and the Czech Republic.

With all its changes in style and pace, basketball's rules and dimensions had changed very little since James Naismith invented the game in 1891. All but one of his 13 original rules were still in effect. Naismith once wrote, "each game has its own evolution that is somewhat independent of the [printed] rules . . ."

In every respect, Naismith's efforts to find something for his bored YMCA gym students to do on a winter's day had indeed come a long way.

CHRONOLOGY

1891	Dr. James Naismith of the Springfield, Massachusetts, YMCA invents the game of basketball.
1893	The first college basketball team is formed at Vanderbilt University.
1895	The scoring system of two points for a field goal and one point for a free throw is adopted.
1896	The first professional game is played at Trenton, New Jersey.
1898	The National Basketball League, the first pro league, is formed. It lasts until 1903.
1914	The Original Celtics organize in New York.
1926	Abe Saperstein creates the Harlem Globetrotters.
1929	All restrictions on dribbling are eliminated, except for the double dribble.
1936	Basketball is added as an Olympic sport.
1940	Kenny Sailors of the University of Wyoming becomes the first player to use a jump shot.
1937	The National Basketball League is founded.
1945	Oklahoma A&M's Bob Kurland becomes the first player to use the dunk as an offensive weapon.
1949	The three-year-old Basketball Association of America and National Basketball League merge to form the 17-team National Basketball Association.
1956	Nine-year-old Lew Alcindor grabs a rebound in a youth game, and out of desperation, throws up his first hook shot, a play that would change the future of basketball.
1967	The American Basketball Association starts play; in 1976 it folds and four teams join the NBA.
1979	The NBA adopts the three-point shot.
1984	The NBA expands the playoffs to allow 16 teams into the postseason.

NBA'S ALL-TIME GREATS

In 1996–97, the NBA celebrated its 50th anniversary by selecting its all-time team.

CENTERS

Kareem Abdul-Jabbar: NBA's all-time leading scorer. Hall of Fame 1995.

Wilt Chamberlain: Most dominating player in history. Hall of Fame 1978.

Dave Cowens: Fiery 6' 9" competitor. Hall of Fame 1991.

Patrick Ewing: Inside player with intimidating blocking ability.

Elvin Hayes: Master of the turnaround jumper. Hall of Fame 1990.

Moses Malone: First to go from high school to the pros.

George Mikan: Basketball's first superstar. Hall of Fame 1959.

Hakeem Olajuwon: Cat-quick 7-footer with low-post power moves.

Shaquille O'Neal: Muscular 7-footer with powerful inside game.

Robert Parish: Played more seasons (22) and games than anyone.

Bob Pettit: Sweet-shooting pivotman. Hall of Fame 1970.

Willis Reed: Spirited floor leader of the Knicks. Hall of Fame 1981.

David Robinson: A top shot blocker with a 23-point average.

Bill Russell: Best of the rebounders and shot blockers. Hall of Fame 1974.

Nate Thurmond: First to record a quadruple double. Hall of Fame 1984.

Wes Unseld: Known for vicious screens and rebounding. Hall of Fame 1988.

Bill Walton: High scorer and strong defensive player. Hall of Fame 1993.

FORWARDS

Paul Arizin: Prolific scorer known as "Pitching Paul." Hall of Fame 1977.

Charles Barkley: Bruising and intimidating power player.

Rick Barry: Deadly outside and one of the greatest free throw shooters. Hall of Fame 1985.

Larry Bird: One of the game's all-time best shooters. Hall of Fame 1997.

Billy Cunningham: Brilliant leaper and rebounder. Hall of Fame 1986.

Dave DeBusschere: Durable, rugged defensive wiz. Hall of Fame 1982.

Clyde Drexler: Versatile forward-guard with breakaway speed.

Julius Erving: Doctor of spinning, leaping, high-flying moves. Hall of Fame 1993.

John Havlicek: Heart and soul of the Celtics for 16 years. Hall of Fame 1983.

Jerry Lucas: Tenacious rebounding overshadowed scoring ability. Hall of Fame 1979.

Kevin McHale: Master of pump fakes, shovel shots, and fadeaway jumpers.

Scottie Pippen: Integral swing player of Chicago Bulls' champions of 1990s.

Dolph Schayes: Played in 706 consecutive games. Hall of Fame 1972.

James Worthy: Known for sweeping dunks, speed, and agility.

GUARDS

Nate "Tiny" Archibald: Led NBA in scoring and assists in one season. Hall of Fame 1991.

Elgin Baylor: The man with a thousand moves. Hall of Fame 1976.

Dave Bing: Graceful, fluid playmaker. Hall of Fame 1989.

Bob Cousy: Greatest playmaker of his era. Hall of Fame 1970.

Walt Frazier: Called "Clyde" for his cool demeanor on the court. Hall of Fame 1987.

George Gervin: Smooth, unstoppable "Ice Man." Hall of Fame 1996.

Hal Greer: Stalwart of great 76ers teams of the 1960s. Hall of Fame 1981.

Earvin "Magic" Johnson: Combination of speed, shooting, passing, and rebounding.

Sam Jones: Could run the floor, hit the boards, and score. Hall of Fame 1983.

Michael Jordan: Greatest player in the history of the game.

"Pistol" Pete Maravich: Master of no-look passes and fall-away jumpers. Hall of Fame 1987.

Earl "The Pearl" Monroe: Twisting, faking, spin-dribbling moves. Hall of Fame 1990.

Oscar Robertson: Versatile player who changed the point guard position. Hall of Fame 1979.

Bill Sharman: Won NBA titles as a player and coach. Hall of Fame 1975.

John Stockton: All-time leader in steals and assists.

Jerry West: Top clutch shooter. Hall of Fame 1979.

Lenny Wilkens: Great passer and floor leader. Hall of Fame (player) 1988.

COACHES

Red Auerbach: Considered greatest coach in NBA history. Hall of Fame 1968.

Phil Jackson: Highest winning percentage in NBA.

Jack Ramsay: Coached 20 years. Hall of Fame 1992.

Pat Riley: Reached 800 wins faster than any coach.

Lenny Wilkens: NBA's all-time winningest coach. Hall of Fame (coach) 1990.

MAJOR RECORDS

INDIVIDUAL

Game

    Points: Wilt Chamberlain, 100

    Rebounds: Wilt Chamberlain, 55

    Playoff Points: Michael Jordan, 63

    Free Throws: Bob Cousy, 30 of 32

    Assists: Scott Skiles, 30

    Blocked Shots: Elmore Smith, 17

Career

    Free Throws: Moses Malone, 8,531

    Points: Kareem Abdul-Jabbar, 38,307

    Points Average: Michael Jordan, 32

    Consecutive Games Played: Randy Smith, 906

TEAM

Consecutive Wins: Los Angeles Lakers, 33 (1971–72)

Most Points, Game: Detroit Pistons, 186

Consecutive Losses: Vancouver, 23 (1995–96)

Points Per Game: Denver Nuggets, 126.5 (1981–82)

Wins in a Season: Chicago Bulls, 72 (1995–96)

FURTHER READING

Anderson, Dave. *The Story of Basketball.* New York: W. Morrow, 1988.

Clary, Jack. *Basketball's Greatest Moments.* New York: McGraw-Hill, 1988.

Marx, Doug. *NBA Champion.* Vero Beach, FL: Rourke Corp, 1992.

Pluto, Terry. *Tall Tales: The Glory Years of the NBA.* New York: Simon & Schuster, 1992.

Ryan, Bob. *The Boston Celtics.* Reading, MA: Addison-Wesley, 1990.

Sachare, Alex, ed. *Official NBA Basketball Encyclopedia.* New York: Villard Books, 1994.

Shapiro, Mike. *Bill Russell.* New York: Chelsea House, 1991.

DENNIS R. TUTTLE, a native of Walnut Cove, N.C., began his sportswriting career at age 17 at his hometown paper, the *Winston-Salem Journal*, in 1977. He has also been a writer and editor at the *Cincinnati Enquirer*, *Austin American-Statesman*, *Knoxville Journal*, and *Washington Times*. He is a two-time winner of an Associated Press Sports Editor's Award for sportswriting excellence. His work has appeared in *The Sporting News*, *USA Today Baseball Weekly*, *Baseball America*, *Inside Sports*, *Washingtonian*, and *Tuff Stuff* magazines. He authored *Juan Gonzalez, Albert Belle* and the *Composite Guide to Football* for Chelsea House. He resides in Cheverly, Maryland.

INDEX

PICTURE CREDITS UPI/Corbis-Bettmann: pp. 2, 6, 9, 22, 24, 27, 37, 40, 45; Basketball Hall of Fame: pp. 12, 15, 21; Library of Congress: p. 14; National Archives: pp. 18, 28, 48, 58; Boston Public Library: p. 30; Corbis-Bettmann: p. 32; Reuters/Corbis-Bettmann: p. 50; AP/Wide World Photos: p. 53; Archive Photos: p. 56